the

NOBEL
LECTURE

BOB DYLAN

Simon & Schuster

London   New York   Toronto   Sydney   New Delhi

First published in the United States by Simon & Schuster, Inc., 2017
First published in Great Britain by Simon & Schuster UK Ltd, 2017
A CBS COMPANY

1 3 5 7 9 10 8 6 4 2

Simon & Schuster UK Ltd
1st Floor
222 Gray's Inn Road
London WC1X 8HB

www.simonandschuster.co.uk
www.simonandschuster.com.au
www.simonandschuster.co.in

Simon & Schuster Australia, Sydney
Simon & Schuster India, New Delhi

A CIP catalogue record for this book is available
from the British Library

Hardback ISBN: 978-1-4711-7218-2
eBook ISBN: 978-1-4711-7219-9

Printed and bound in Italy by L.E.G.O. S.p.A.

the

NOBEL LECTURE

When I received the Nobel Prize for Literature, I got to wondering exactly how my songs related to literature. I wanted to reflect on it and see where the connection was. I'm going to try to articulate that to you. And most likely it will go in a roundabout way, but I hope what I say will be worthwhile and purposeful.

If I was to go back to the dawning of it all, I guess I'd have to start with Buddy Holly. Buddy died when I was about eighteen and he was twenty-two. From the moment I first heard him, I felt akin. I felt related, like he was an older brother. I even thought I resembled him. Buddy played the music that I loved—the music I grew up on: country western, rock 'n' roll, and rhythm and blues. Three separate strands of music that he intertwined and infused into one genre. One brand. And Buddy wrote songs—songs that had beautiful melodies and imaginative verses. And he sang great—sang in more than a few

BOB DYLAN

voices. He was the archetype. Everything I wasn't and wanted to be. I saw him only but once, and that was a few days before he was gone. I had to travel a hundred miles to get to see him play, and I wasn't disappointed.

He was powerful and electrifying and had a commanding presence. I was only six feet away. He was mesmerizing. I watched his face, his hands, the way he tapped his foot, his big black glasses, the eyes behind the glasses, the way he held his guitar, the way he stood, his neat suit. Everything about him. He looked older than twenty-two. Something about him seemed permanent, and he filled me with conviction. Then, out of the blue, the most uncanny thing happened. He looked me right straight dead in the eye, and he transmitted something. Something I didn't know what. And it gave me the chills.

I think it was a day or two after that, that his plane went down. And somebody—somebody I'd never seen before—handed me a Leadbelly record with the song "Cotton Fields" on it. And that record changed my life right then and there. Transported me into a world I'd never known. It was like an explosion went off. Like I'd been walking in darkness and all of a sudden the darkness was illuminated. It was like somebody laid hands on me. I must have played that record a hundred times.

It was on a label I'd never heard of with a booklet inside with advertisements for other artists on the label: Sonny Terry and Brownie McGhee, the New Lost City Ramblers, Jean Ritchie, string bands. I'd never heard of any of them. But I reckoned if they were on this label with Leadbelly, they had to be good, so I needed to hear them. I wanted to know all about it and play that kind of music. I still had a feeling for the music I'd grown up with, but for right now, I forgot about it. Didn't even think about it. For the time being, it was long gone.

I hadn't left home yet, but I couldn't wait to. I wanted to learn this music and meet the people who played it. Eventually, I did leave, and I did learn to play those songs. They were different than the radio songs that I'd been listening to all along. They were more vibrant and truthful to life. With radio songs, a performer might get a hit with a roll of the dice or a fall of the cards, but that didn't matter in the folk world. Everything was a hit. All you had to do was be well versed and be able to play the melody. Some of these songs were easy, some not. I had a natural feeling for the ancient ballads and country blues, but everything else I had to learn from scratch. And I was playing for small crowds, sometimes no more than four or five people in a room or on a street corner. You had to have a wide repertoire, and you had to know what to play and when. Some songs were intimate, some you had to shout to be heard.

By listening to all the early folk artists and singing the songs yourself, you pick up the vernacular. You internalize it. You sing it in the ragtime blues, work songs, Georgia sea shanties, Appalachian ballads, and cowboy songs. You hear all the finer points, and you learn the details.

You know what it's all about. Takin' the pistol

out and puttin' it back in your pocket. Whippin' your way through traffic, talkin' in the dark. You know that Stagger Lee was a bad man and that Frankie was a good girl. You know that Washington is a bourgeois town and you've heard the deep-pitched voice of John the Revelator and you saw the *Titanic* sink in a boggy creek. And you're pals with the wild Irish rover and the wild colonial boy. You heard the muffled drums and the fifes that played lowly. You've seen the lusty Lord Donald stick a knife in his wife, and a lot of your comrades have been wrapped in white linen.

I had all the vernacular down. I knew the rhetoric. None of it went over my head—the devices, the techniques, the secrets, the mysteries—and I knew all the deserted roads that it traveled on, too. I could make it all connect and move with the current of the day. When I started writing my own songs the folk lingo was the only vocabulary that I knew, and I used it.

But I had something else as well. I had principles and sensibilities and an informed view of the world. And I had had that for a while. Learned it all in grammar school. *Don Quixote*, *Ivanhoe*, *Robinson Crusoe*, *Gulliver's Travels*, *Tale of Two Cities*, all the rest—typical grammar school reading that gave you a way of looking at life, an understanding of human nature, and a standard to measure things by. I took all that with me when I started composing lyrics. And the themes from those books worked their way into many of my songs, either knowingly or unintentionally. I wanted to write songs unlike anything anybody ever heard, and these themes were fundamental.

Specific books that have stuck with me ever since I read them way back in grammar school— I want to tell you about three of them: *Moby-Dick*, *All Quiet on the Western Front*, and *The Odyssey*.

Moby-Dick is a fascinating book, a book that's filled with scenes of high drama and dramatic dialogue.

The book makes demands on you. The plot is straightforward. The mysterious Captain Ahab—captain of a ship called the *Pequod*—an egomaniac with a peg leg pursuing his nemesis, the great white whale Moby-Dick, who took his leg. And he pursues him all the way from the Atlantic around the tip of Africa and into the Indian Ocean. He pursues the whale around both sides of the earth. It's an abstract goal, nothing concrete or definite. He calls Moby the emperor, sees him as the embodiment of evil. Ahab's got a wife and child back in Nantucket that he reminisces about now and again. You can anticipate what will happen.

The ship's crew is made up of men of different races, and any one of them who sights the whale will be given the reward of a gold coin. A lot of zodiac symbols, religious allegory, stereotypes. Ahab encounters other whaling vessels, presses the captains for details about Moby. Have they seen him? There's a crazy prophet, Gabriel, on one of the vessels, and he predicts Ahab's doom. Says Moby is the incarnate of a Shaker god, and that any dealings with him will lead to disaster. He says that to Captain Ahab. Another ship's captain—Captain Boomer— he lost an arm to Moby. But he tolerates that, and he's happy to have survived. He can't accept Ahab's lust for vengeance.

This book tells how different men react in different ways to the same experience. A lot of Old Testament, biblical allegory: Gabriel, Rachel, Jeroboam, Bildad, Elijah. Pagan names as well: Tashtego, Flask, Daggoo, Fleece, Starbuck, Stubb, Martha's Vineyard. The pagans are idol worshippers. Some worship little wax figures, some wooden figures. Some worship fire. The *Pequod* is the name of an Indian tribe.

Moby-Dick is a seafaring tale. One of the men, the narrator, says, "Call me Ishmael." Somebody asks him where he's from, and he says, "It's not down on any map. True places never are." Stubb gives no significance to anything, says everything is predestined. Ishmael's been on a sailing ship his entire life. Calls the sailing ships his Harvard and Yale. He keeps his distance from people.

A typhoon hits the *Pequod*. Captain Ahab thinks it's a good omen. Starbuck thinks it's a bad omen, considers killing Ahab. As soon as the storm ends, a crew member falls from the ship's mast and drowns, foreshadowing what's to come. A Quaker pacifist priest, who is actually a bloodthirsty businessman, tells Flask some men who receive injuries are led to God, others are led to bitterness.

Everything is mixed in. All the myths: the Judeo-Christian Bible, Hindu myths, British legends, Saint George, Perseus, Hercules—they're all whalers. Greek mythology, the gory business of cutting up a whale. Lots of facts in this book, geographical knowledge, whale oil—good for coronation of royalty—noble families in the whaling industry. Whale oil is used to anoint the kings. History of the whale, phrenology, classical philosophy, pseudoscientific theories, justification for discrimination—everything thrown in and none of it hardly rational. Highbrow, lowbrow, chasing illusion, chasing death, the great white whale, white as a polar bear, white as a white man, the emperor, the nemesis, the embodiment of evil. The demented captain who actually lost his leg years ago trying to attack Moby with a knife.

We see only the surface of things. We can interpret what lies below any way we see fit. Crewmen walk around on deck listening for mermaids, and sharks and vultures follow the ship. Reading skulls and faces like you read a book. Here's a face. I'll put it in front of you. Read it if you can.

Tashtego says that he died and was reborn. His extra days are a gift. He wasn't saved by Christ, though, he says he was saved by a fellow man and a non-Christian at that. He parodies the Resurrection.

When Starbuck tells Ahab that he should let bygones be bygones, the angry captain snaps back, "Speak not to me of blasphemy, man, I'd strike the sun if it insulted me." Ahab, too, is a poet of eloquence. He says, "The path to my fixed purpose is laid with iron rails whereon my soul is grooved to run." Or these lines: "All visible objects are but pasteboard masks." Quotable poetic phrases that can't be beat.

Finally, Ahab spots Moby, and the harpoons come out. Boats are lowered. Ahab's harpoon has been baptized in blood. Moby attacks Ahab's boat and destroys it. Next day, he sights Moby again. Boats are lowered again. Moby attacks Ahab's boat again. On the third day, another boat goes in. More religious allegory. He has risen. Moby attacks one more time, ramming the *Pequod* and sinking it. Ahab gets tangled up in the harpoon lines and is thrown out of his boat into a watery grave.

Ishmael survives. He's in the sea floating on a coffin. And that's about it. That's the whole story. That theme and all that it implies would work its way into more than a few of my songs.

All Quiet on the Western Front was another book that did. *All Quiet on the Western Front* is a horror story.

This is a book where you lose your childhood, your faith in a meaningful world, and your concern for individuals. You're stuck in a nightmare. Sucked up into a mysterious whirlpool of death and pain. You're defending yourself from elimination. You're being wiped off the face of the map. Once upon a time you were an innocent youth with big dreams about being a concert pianist. Once you loved life and the world, and now you're shooting it to pieces.

Day after day, the hornets bite you and worms lap your blood. You're a cornered animal. You don't fit anywhere. The falling rain is monotonous. There's endless assaults, poison gas, nerve gas, morphine, burning streams of gasoline, scavenging and scabbing for food, influenza, typhus, dysentery. Life is breaking down all around you, and the shells are whistling. This is the lower region of hell. Mud, barbed wire, rat-filled trenches, rats eating the intestines of dead men, trenches filled with filth and excrement. Someone shouts, "Hey, you there. Stand and fight."

Who knows how long this mess will go on? Warfare has no limits. You're being annihilated, and that leg of yours is bleeding too much. You killed a man yesterday, and you spoke to his corpse. You told him after this is over, you'll spend the rest of your life looking after his family. Who's profiting here? The leaders and the generals gain fame, and many others profit financially. But you're doing the dirty work. One of your comrades says, "Wait a minute, where are you going?" And you say, "Leave me alone, I'll be back in a minute." Then you walk out into the woods of death hunting for a piece of sausage. You can't see how anybody in civilian life has any kind of purpose at all. All their worries, all their desires—you can't comprehend it.

More machine guns rattle, more parts of bodies hanging from wires, more pieces of arms and legs and skulls where butterflies perch on teeth, more hideous wounds, pus coming out of every pore, lung wounds, wounds too big for the body, gas-blowing cadavers, and dead bodies making retching noises. Death is everywhere. Nothing else is possible. Someone will kill you and use your dead body for target practice. Boots, too. They're your prized possession. But soon they'll be on somebody else's feet.

There's Froggies coming through the trees. Merciless bastards. Your shells are running out. "It's not fair to come at us again so soon," you say. One of your companions is lying in the dirt, and you want to take him to the field hospital. Someone else says, "You might save yourself a trip." "What do you mean?" "Turn him over, you'll see what I mean."

You wait to hear the news. You don't understand why the war isn't over. The army is so strapped for replacement troops that they're drafting young boys who are of little military use, but they're draftin' 'em anyway because they're running out of men. Sickness and humiliation have broken your heart. You were betrayed by your parents, your schoolmasters, your ministers, and even your own government.

The general with the slowly smoked cigar betrayed you, too—turned you into a thug and a murderer. If you could, you'd put a bullet in his face. The commander as well. You fantasize that if you had the money, you'd put up a reward for any man who would take his life by any means necessary. And if he should lose his life by doing that, then let the money go to his heirs. The colonel, too, with his caviar and his coffee—he's another one. Spends all his time in the officers' brothel. You'd like to see him stoned dead, too. More Tommies and Johnnies with their whack fo' me daddy-o and their whiskey in the jars. You kill twenty of 'em and twenty more will spring up in their place. It just stinks in your nostrils.

You've come to despise that older generation that sent you out into this madness, into this torture chamber. All around you, your comrades are dying. Dying from abdominal wounds, double amputations, shattered hip bones, and you think, "I'm only twenty years old, but I'm capable of killing anybody. Even my father if he came at me."

Yesterday, you tried to save a wounded messenger dog, and somebody shouted, "Don't be a fool." One Froggy is lying gurgling at your feet. You stuck him with a dagger in his stomach, but the man still lives. You know you should finish the job, but you can't. You're on the real iron cross, and a Roman soldier's putting a sponge of vinegar to your lips.

Months pass by. You go home on leave. You can't communicate with your father. He said, "You'd be a coward if you don't enlist." Your mother, too, on your way back out the door, she says, "You be careful of those French girls now." More madness. You fight for a week or a month, and you gain ten yards. And then the next month it gets taken back.

All that culture from a thousand years ago, that philosophy, that wisdom—Plato, Aristotle, Socrates—what happened to it? It should have prevented this. Your thoughts turn homeward. And once again you're a schoolboy walking through the tall poplar trees. It's a pleasant memory. More bombs dropping on you from blimps. You got to get it together now. You can't even look at anybody for fear of some miscalculable thing that might happen. The common grave. There are no other possibilities.

Then you notice the cherry blossoms, and you see that nature is unaffected by all this. Poplar trees, the red butterflies, the fragile beauty of flowers, the sun—you see how nature is indifferent to it all. All the violence and suffering of mankind. Nature doesn't even notice it.

You're so alone. Then a piece of shrapnel hits the side of your head and you're dead. You've been ruled out, crossed out. You've been exterminated. I put this book down and closed it up. I never wanted to read another war novel again, and I never did.

Charlie Poole from North Carolina had a song that connected to all this. It's called "You Ain't Talkin' to Me," and the lyrics go like this:

I saw a sign in the window walking up town one
    day.

Join the army, see the world is what it had to say.

You'll see exciting places with a jolly crew,

You'll meet interesting people, and learn to kill
    them too.

Oh you ain't talkin' to me, you ain't talking to me.

I may be crazy and all that, but I got good sense
    you see.

You ain't talkin' to me, you ain't talkin' to me.

Killin' with a gun don't sound like fun.

You ain't talkin' to me.

The Odyssey is a great book whose themes have
worked their way into the ballads of a lot of songwriters: "Homeward Bound," "Green, Green Grass of
Home," "Home on the Range," and my songs as well.

    The Odyssey is a strange, adventurous tale of a
grown man trying to get home after fighting in a war.
He's on that long journey home, and it's filled with

traps and pitfalls. He's cursed to wander. He's always getting carried out to sea, always having close calls. Huge chunks of boulders rock his boat. He angers people he shouldn't. There's troublemakers in his crew. Treachery. His men are turned into pigs and then are turned back into younger, more handsome men. He's always trying to rescue somebody. He's a travelin' man, but he's making a lot of stops.

He's stranded on a desert island. He finds deserted caves, and he hides in them. He meets giants that say, "I'll eat you last." And he escapes from giants. He's trying to get back home, but he's tossed and turned by the winds. Restless winds, chilly winds, unfriendly winds. He travels far, and then he gets blown back.

He's always being warned of things to come. Touching things he's told not to. There's two roads to take, and they're both bad. Both hazardous. On one you could drown and on the other you could starve. He goes into the narrow straits with foaming whirlpools that swallow him. Meets six-headed monsters with sharp fangs. Thunderbolts strike at him. Overhanging branches that he makes a leap to reach for to save himself from a raging river. Goddesses and gods protect him, but some others want to kill him. He changes identities. He's exhausted. He falls asleep, and he's woken up by the sound of laughter. He tells his story to strangers. He's been gone twenty years. He was carried off somewhere and left there. Drugs have been dropped into his wine. It's been a hard road to travel.

In a lot of ways, some of these same things have happened to you. You too have had drugs dropped into your wine. You too have shared a bed with the wrong woman. You too have been spellbound by magical voices, sweet voices with strange melodies. You too have come so far and have been so far blown back. And you've had close calls as well. You have angered people you should not have. And you too have rambled this country all around. And you've also felt that ill wind, the wind that blows you no good. And that's still not all of it.

When he gets back home, things aren't any better. Scoundrels have moved in and are taking advantage of his wife's hospitality. And there's too many of 'em. And though he's greater than them all and the best at everything—best carpenter, best hunter, best expert on animals, best seaman—his courage won't save him, but his trickery will.

All these stragglers will have to pay for desecrating his palace. He'll disguise himself as a filthy beggar, and a lowly servant kicks him down the steps with arrogance and stupidity. The servant's arrogance revolts him, but he controls his anger. He's one against a hundred, but they'll all fall, even the strongest. He was nobody. And when it's all said and done, when he's home at last, he sits with his wife, and he tells her the stories.

So what does it all mean? Myself and a lot of other songwriters have been influenced by these very same themes. And they can mean a lot of different things.

If a song moves you, that's all that's important. I don't have to know what a song means. I've written all kinds of things into my songs. And I'm not going to worry about it—what it all means. When Melville put all his Old Testament, biblical references, scientific theories, Protestant doctrines, and all that knowledge of the sea and sailing ships and whales into one story, I don't think he would have worried about it either—what it all means.

John Donne as well, the poet-priest who lived in the time of Shakespeare, wrote these words: "The Sestos and Abydos of her breasts. Not of two lovers, but two loves, the nests." I don't know what it means, either. But it sounds good. And you want your songs to sound good.

When Odysseus in *The Odyssey* visits the famed warrior Achilles in the underworld, Achilles—who traded a long life full of peace and contentment for a short one full of honor and glory—tells Odysseus it was all a mistake. "I just died, that's all." There was no honor. No immortality. And that if he could, he would choose to go back and be a lowly slave to a tenant farmer on earth rather than be what he is, a king in the land of the dead. That whatever his struggles of life were, they were preferable to being here in this dead place.

And that's what songs are, too. Our songs are alive in the land of the living. But songs are unlike literature. They're meant to be sung, not read. The words in Shakespeare's plays were meant to be acted on the stage. Just as lyrics in songs are meant to be sung, not read on a page. And I hope some of you get the chance to listen to these lyrics the way they were intended to be heard: in concert or on record or however people are listening to songs these days. I return once again to Homer, who says, "Sing in me, O Muse, and through me tell the story."

ABOUT THE AUTHOR

Bob Dylan has released thirty-eight studio albums, which collectively have sold over 120 million copies around the world. He won the Nobel Prize in Literature and has been awarded the French Legion of Honor, a Pulitzer Prize Special Citation, a doctorate from Scotland's University of St. Andrews, and the Presidential Medal of Freedom, the country's highest civilian honor. His memoir, *Chronicles: Volume One*, spent a year on the *New York Times* bestseller list.